American Clematis Society's

Guide to Growing

CLEMATIS

in the United States

By

Edith M. Malek

Published by the American Clematis Society
P.O. Box 17085
Irvine, CA 92623-7085

ISBN 0-9670538-0-3
Text and photographs copyright © 1999 Edith M. Malek

First Printing 1999

Printed in the U.S.A.

Table of Contents

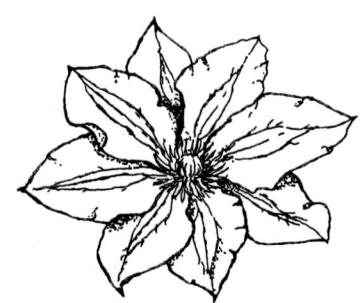

Acknowledgments

I would like to thank my sweet mother, Stella Askew and my loving husband, Ken Malek
for their patience in editing this book and their continual love and belief in me.

I also want to thank my two wonderful children, Anthony and Emily Malek
for their love while I did this project.

I want to thank all my loyal ACS members for their tremendous ongoing
support and encouragement.

And special thanks to John Gibbons, Jo Standifer and Blanche Uyema
for being there when I needed them.

Introduction

This is the first publication devoted to growing Clematis in the United States. I have made it my life's ambition to make this beautiful and versatile plant as "Recognizable as the Rose" in America. I hope that the contents of this book will help to achieve that goal.

Clematis forever!

Edith M. Malek

Edith M. Malek
(AKA the 'Clematis Queen' to my loyal subjects)

Endorsements by the American Clematis Society

The American Clematis Society endorses various products that it feels are exceptional and will be advantageous for gardeners to successfully grow Clematis in the United States. However, since the horticultural world is constantly changing because of government requirements, new innovations, and growing improvements, we have not mentioned them by name in this book. For current information on these endorsed products please visit our Website or send a self-addressed stamped envelope for a list.

klem' ∂-tis

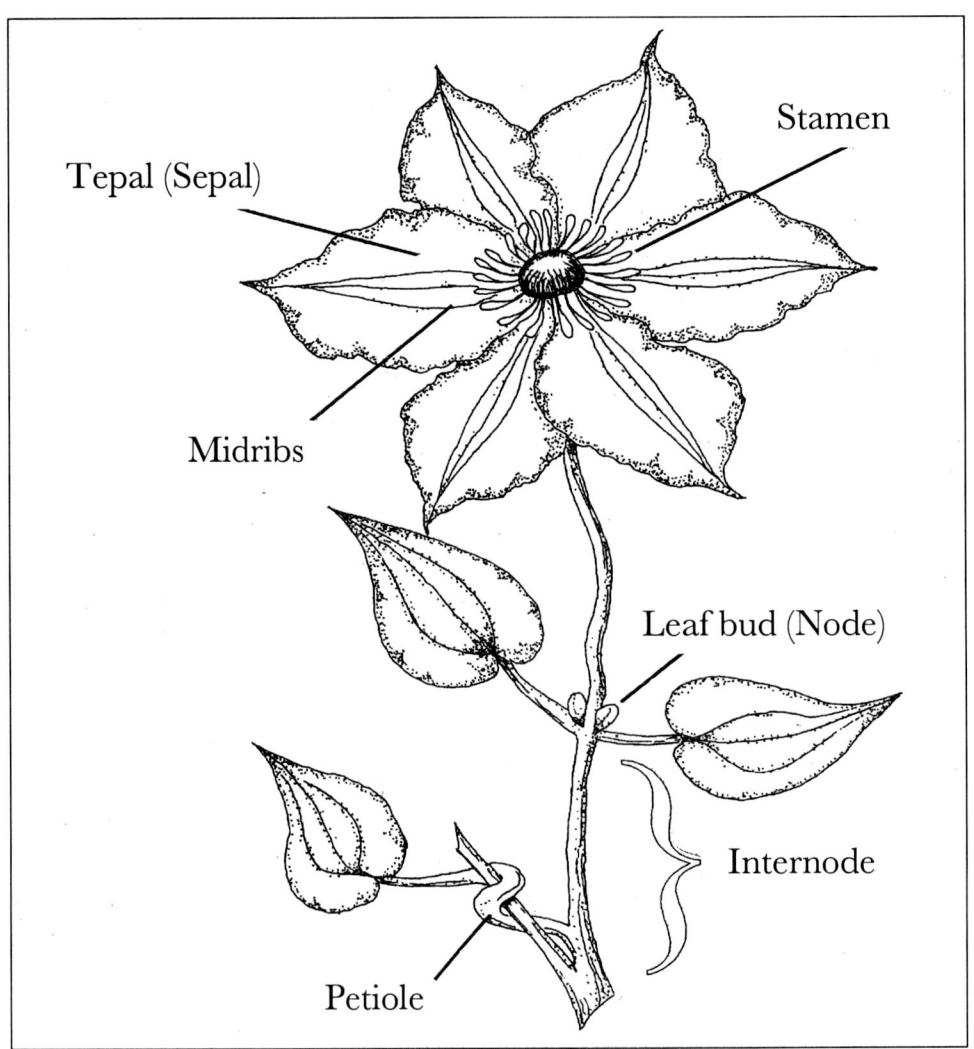

Tepal (Sepal)

Stamen

Midribs

Leaf bud (Node)

Internode

Petiole

Clematis (klem' ∂-tis) is the Greek word for some kind of climbing or trailing plant and the correct pronunciation is CLEM-uh-tis. Clematis belongs to the Ranunculaceae (Buttercup) family. Clematis is a genus of over 200 species and at least 1000 cultivars. Most Clematis are described as deciduous, woody climbers. Some other family members are Anemones, Aquilegia, Delphiniums, Hellebores and Larkspur. There are a few evergreen Clematis such as Clematis armandii and Clematis cirrhosa as well as several erect herbaceous perennial Clematis such as Clematis integrifolia and Clematis recta.

One thing to remember is that Clematis are ugly in the winter. They look as if they are dead. I feel though, that the beauty that they bring us the rest of year far outweighs this one minor flaw that can easily be overlooked.

Tepals or Sepals?

There is some confusion as to whether you should call the petal-like structure tepals or sepals. If you read any of the earlier books on Clematis they are referred to as sepals. When you read the current books on Clematis, you see a growing trend to call them tepals. Presently, using tepal or sepal is correct. I have decided to refer to them as tepals in this book because I believe that this term will eventually be considered the correct one.

You may have noticed that I have used the term petal-like. This is because, in reality, Clematis have no true petals. The colored segments of the flower are in fact tepals.

Color of Clematis

Many factors can affect the coloring of the blooms on your Clematis from one season to the next or even from day to day. Things such as how long a flower has been in bloom, exposure to sunlight and weather, and the time of the year can determine how intense the colors of your flowers will be. Each of these conditions can affect different Clematis in varying degrees.

For example, the Clematis 'Niobe' has an almost black tinge when it opens. It gradually lightens through a deep magenta red to a softer and still attractive magenta. The vivid pink bars of the 'Nelly Moser' when grown in bright sunlight, will rapidly fade. Also, climatic conditions can dictate color intensity. Because 'Asao' is one of the first Clematis to bloom early in the year, when the weather is colder, their first crop of blooms is deeper in color. Subsequent blooming cycles will produce lighter-colored flowers.

It is important to know that, even though Clematis are listed as 'red' or 'blue', there are no *true* reds or blues. Red Clematis always have a magenta cast. You will not find fire-engine red because all of the reds contain a blue hue to their coloration. Blue Clematis are never really sky or royal blue. They always contain purple tints, closer to periwinkle blue or purplish-blue.

How Clematis Attach Themselves

Clematis are resourceful plants that can attach themselves to other plants as well as support structures. Clematis are equipped with a delicate leaf stem, which is called a 'petiole'. These petioles have tendril-like qualities, which are able to twist around something, allowing them to latch on to things as they grow. Unlike tendrils, their embrace is not a death grip but is more relaxed and can be removed. Even though nature has provided Clematis with this unique ability, they will still need a helping hand. They may need some tying and training.

Where to Plant Your Clematis

Choosing the best planting site for your Clematis involves three major considerations. The first is interpreting the zone map. Next is finding the perfect spot paying special attention to exposure to the sun. Finally, understanding what pH means. We will discuss these subjects separately, although, of course, they must all work together in order to produce breathtakingly beautiful Clematis plants that will be your pride and joy and the envy of everyone else.

This book uses the generally accepted climate zones of the _Official USDA Plant Hardiness Zone Map_, (see page 9) which was revised in 1986. At that time a new zone–zone 11–was introduced, representing areas that are essentially frost-free. But since only <u>minimum</u> temperatures are taken into account on the USDA map, it should only be used as a guideline. Because zone maps do not show heat, humidity or other factors that could affect your plant, many microclimates may exist within a zone. It may be possible, for example, for zone 4 conditions to exist within zone 3.

I believe that the zones 4 through 11 are the most favorable areas for growing Clematis. I divide these zones into two categories: zones 4 through 9, which experience lower minimum temperatures, and zones 10 and 11, which have moderate minimum temperatures. The difference between these two categories is important because it will affect how you prune and feed your Clematis.

Clematis are cold-hardy vines that can tolerate minimum temperatures below 30°. They have a high level of success in zones 4 through 9, which are traditionally cold-winter areas. However, contrary to popular belief, they can also thrive in the hotter temperatures associated with zones 10 and 11.

In the unique microclimates of zones 10 and 11, there are no distinct flowering seasons. There tend to be smaller crops of flowers that bloom an extended period of time. Depending on the location and cultivar there can be several cycles in one year. This can be attributed to warm weather and mild winters.

If you live in a zone that experiences very hot weather in the summer months, the safest and easiest to grow would be the varieties of small-flowered hybrid Clematis viticella. Heat is a major concern when growing Clematis, but my own personal experience has shown me that even during Southern California heatwaves, where temperatures above 100 degrees are not uncommon, Clematis can continue to bloom.

Selecting the Best Planting Site

Remember, location is everything! Choosing the perfect spot is critical to a plant's survival. Keep in mind where the edge of the roof is, so that during heavy rainfalls your plant will not be damaged by the drainage. Clematis are also best planted at least four feet away from trees and two to three feet away from shrubs so they will not have to compete with these established

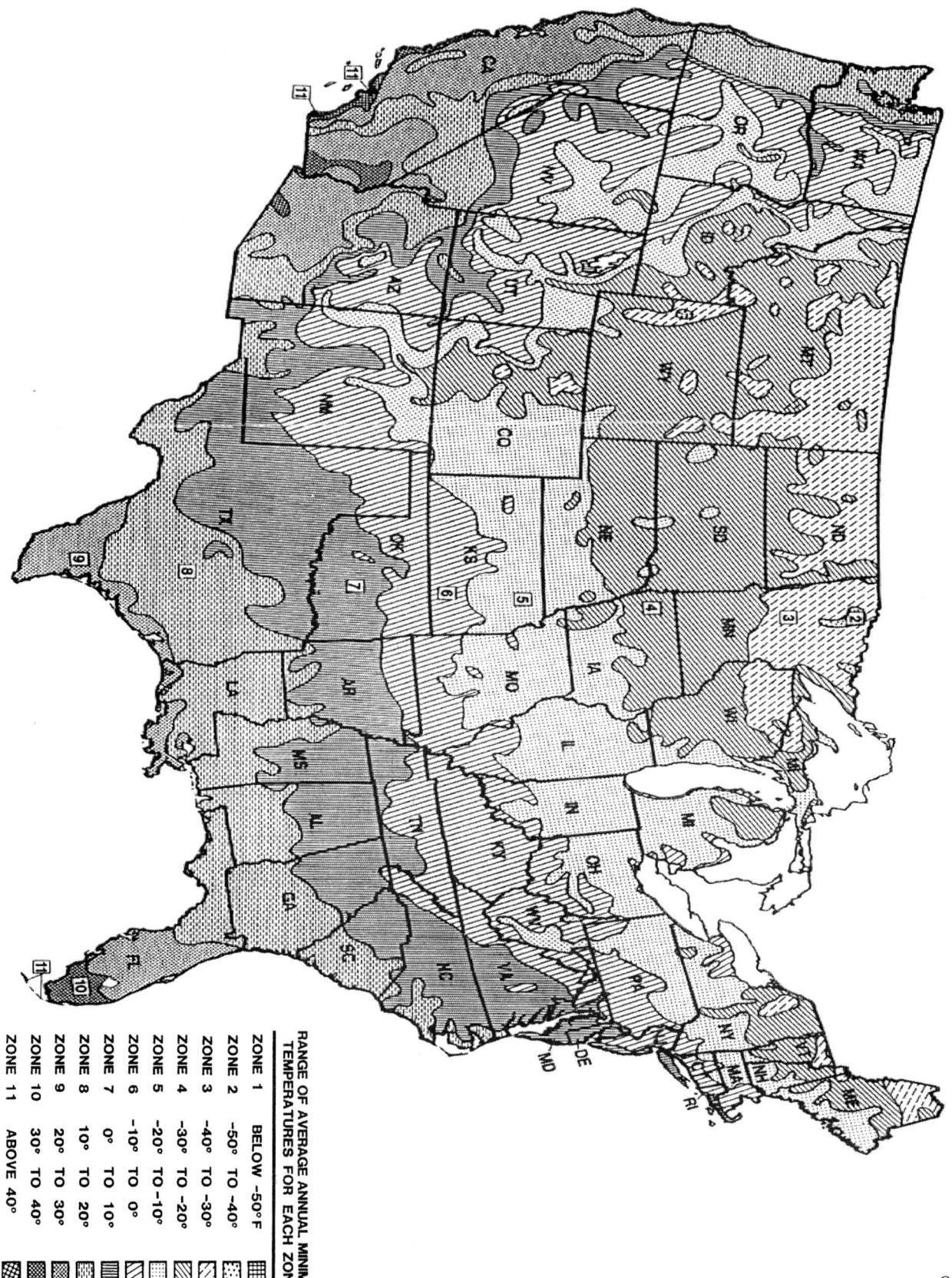

RANGE OF AVERAGE ANNUAL MINIMUM
TEMPERATURES FOR EACH ZONE

ZONE 1	BELOW -50° F
ZONE 2	-50° TO -40°
ZONE 3	-40° TO -30°
ZONE 4	-30° TO -20°
ZONE 5	-20° TO -10°
ZONE 6	-10° TO 0°
ZONE 7	0° TO 10°
ZONE 8	10° TO 20°
ZONE 9	20° TO 30°
ZONE 10	30° TO 40°
ZONE 11	ABOVE 40°

plants for water. These distances still allow you to grow your Clematis with a host plant at a later date or just let it thrive on its own.

The amount of sunlight you provide will also affect the appearance and health of your Clematis. It is important for you to know how much (how many hours) and what kind (direct or diffused) of sunlight you have before you select the proper planting site.

Sunny Exposure

Most Clematis prefer a full-sun location which means they require five to six hours of sunlight in order to produce the fullest amount of blooms.

Sunny locations are best suited for strong colored Clematis, especially the red and purple cultivars, although they can grow in less sunlight. These strong-colored Clematis prefer full sun to bring out their true color. They normally withstand direct sun without fading.

Shady Exposure

Shady locations are best suited for delicate-colored Clematis, especially the light-pinks and soft silvery-lavender cultivars. They do best when planted in <u>bright</u> shade, which can consist of areas that experience partial shade or dappled shade, but never receive direct, continuous sunlight. Direct sunlight bleaches the soft colors of these pale Clematis flowers, leaving them a dingy washed out gray. Bright shady locations are also recommended for extremely hot areas of this country where the scorching summer heat can burn delicate Clematis blooms.

Cultural Requirements

When selecting your planting site you should look for an area that matches Clematis's own natural settings as closely as possible. In their natural environment they grow in an area where their roots are shaded and there is a plentiful supply of water. The soil should be rich with organic matter and well aerated.

The Ideal pH

So, what is pH and what does it mean to your Clematis? pH refers to a scale measuring the acid or alkaline content of your soil. 7.0 is neutral. Anything above 7.0 is considered to be alkaline; anything below 7.0 would be acidic. Clematis, like most of your other garden plants, grow more favorably in a pH of 6.5 to 7.0. Although they will survive in a neutral soil of 7.0, I recommend that the pH range be closer to 6.5. If you are unsure what your pH is you should have your soil tested.

In areas of the U.S. such as Southern California, where there is not a lot of rainfall, you will find high concentrations of alkalinity in the soil. In these areas it is a good gardening practice to add gypsum or gypsite to your garden in the spring and again in the fall, especially if your soil has tested above 7.0. These products will help to reduce the pH of your soil.

Some gardeners believe that you should add lime to the planting site. I am opposed to this practice because I feel that it increases the alkalinity of the soil, which is harmful to Clematis.

The only exception would be if you live in an area that has a _major calcium deficiency_ it may be necessary to add lime. However, you should do this _only_ if you have a professional soil lab test your soil and their findings recommend it.

Choosing Your Clematis

Having picked the perfect spot with the proper light exposure, it's time to choose the perfect plant.

Keys to Buying a Healthy Clematis

Always buy the biggest plant possible. I would not recommend anything smaller than a two-gallon plant. Five-gallon plants are preferable because you are more likely to get a well-established plant with a bigger rootball. You are ensured better results because the wholesale nursery has done the early training for you.

Always look for strong, thick and undamaged stems. This is an absolute must for your plant's survival. The thicker the stems the better!

Always buy a healthy plant. Do not buy a plant just because it's low-priced. When you consider that your Clematis can live up to 30 years, paying top dollar for a plant is still a wise investment. Bargains are wonderful only if combined with finding a healthy plant.

Always buy a named cultivar! Make sure the plant is properly identified by checking that the tag has the full scientific name on it. If the label just says "Purple Clematis", do not buy it! You will have no idea how to prune it or what size it will become.

Always buy from a reputable nursery with a knowledgeable sales staff. Ask questions. If you feel their answers are not adequate find another nurseryperson or go to a different nursery.

Supporting Your Clematis

Being a vine, a Clematis does its best when grown up some type of support whether it is man-made or natural. If you allow your Clematis to grow on the ground, it increases the possibility of attack by enemies such as earwigs, slugs and snails.

Clematis can grow happily up just about anything with only your imagination limiting what you decide to do. They can hide an unsightly chainlink fence, wind around a mailbox post or a lamppost, climb over an arbor or adorn a pergola. The effect of Clematis spilling over a fuchsia frame, topping a porch entrance, gracing an obelisk or framing an alcove can be dramatic. Growing Clematis up one of the beautiful commercial trellises that are available, as well as building your own structures, are other ideas to consider.

Because Clematis do well in containers and grow vertically when properly supported, they are ideal plants for a patio garden or other small area.

Clematis make great companion plants because they intermingle easily with a whole variety of host plants. They will not harm the host plants that are providing them their natural support. Instead, they add to their beauty. Allowing Clematis to sprawl through trees, shrubs, roses, vines and other plants provides them with the added benefit of a perfect microclimate. This reduces the heat in the summer and protects it from the cold in the winter. Another plus is that these host plants can also camouflage the Clematis when they are not looking their best.

It is also a good idea to combine other vines with Clematis when you are growing them on man-made structures. This gives you the best of both worlds, an attractive support structure as well as protective microclimate.

If you are going to use a tree or a large shrub as a support, make sure that you plant your Clematis at least four feet away from the trunk. If you choose a small to medium shrub as the support, you should plant the Clematis two to three feet away. The reason for planting the Clematis a little distance away from the host plant is to give it its own water supply and rooting area. This keeps it from having to be in constant competition with the host plant for water and root space.

To decide which plants to combine with your Clematis, use one of the many Garden Encyclopedias or Regional Gardening Guides to help you pick the plants that are appropriate for your unique growing zone.

Planting Your Clematis

You can do everything else right, up to this point, but if you do not plant your Clematis correctly, all your hard work and effort will have been in vain.

The Best Time to Plant

The ideal times to plant Clematis are in the spring or the fall. In hotter areas of the country, I always suggest waiting for the cooler months before planting. This will help reduce the initial stress to the plant and will allow it to acclimate during the cool season.

Of course Clematis can be planted at any season of the year, but, without special care, the results of doing so could be disastrous. If you decide to plant in the summer months of June, July or August, you will need to water your plants <u>every day</u>. Residents of Zones 10 and 11 can also include the month of September.

If you have acquired your plant in one of these summer months and decide to follow my advice and wait until fall to plant, you should leave your Clematis in its original nursery container and care for it as if you had transplanted it in a container.

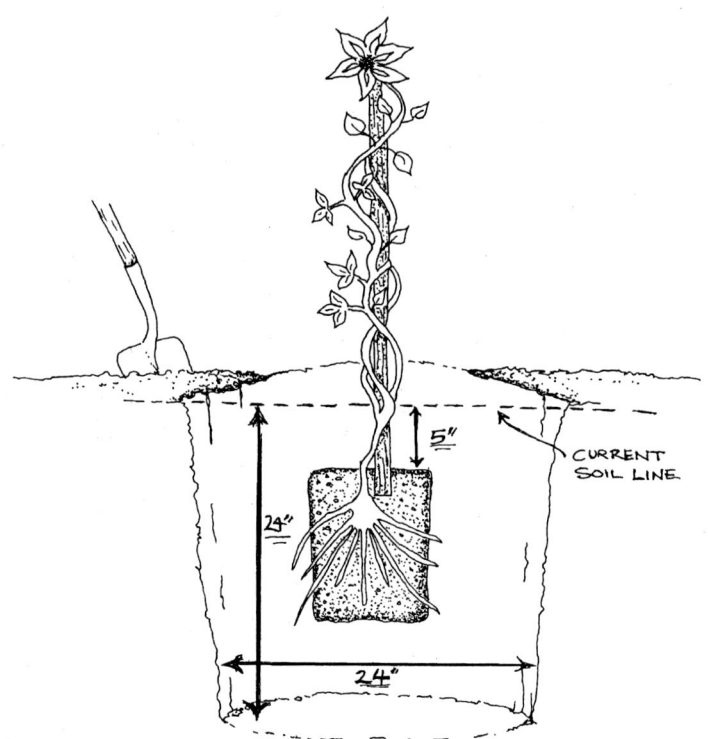

Planting Your New Clematis

Having chosen your planting site, dig a hole a minimum of 18 inches wide by 18 inches deep, preferably 24 inches wide by 24 inches deep. The larger hole not only allows you to add more soil amendment, it also gives the roots of your Clematis more room to roam.

14

The first step in planting must always be preparing the soil. Soil types vary greatly from area to area, but whatever type you are dealing with in your own garden, whether clay, sandy or loam, you will need to add soil amendment before planting your Clematis. Do this by mixing the displaced topsoil from the planting hole with soil amendment in the proportions that I recommend for your soil type, as follows.

If you have clay soil or other heavy soil it already has plenty of moisture-holding ability, but the aeration will need to be improved. Do this by making a mix of 50% high-grade amendment and 50% topsoil.

If you have sandy soil you can improve its moisture-holding ability by adding 30% to 50% high-grade amendment.

If you have loam soil, you have been blessed with the best of all soil types! Even so, adding 20% amendment to your soil would be beneficial.

Cut the can and *carefully* remove the rootball. Never pull it out of the container. If the roots appear rootbound, carefully loosen the outermost roots to encourage proper root distribution. But the fibrous roots of Clematis species are so delicate, I would recommend loosening them only if they are extremely rootbound.

Add a sufficient amount of your amended topsoil to the hole so that when you position your Clematis it will be three inches to five inches below the surface of the soil. Keep adding amended soil until the hole is full. Should your Clematis ever get wilt or suffer any other surface damage, burying it deep gives it a second chance to sprout new stems.

Leave the original support stake or trellis in place until the Clematis has a chance to acclimate to its new home. At that time, remove the old prop and attach the Clematis to its permanent support. Usually this should be done after the first year.

Water the Clematis thoroughly after planting. Use a seaweed extract to help promote root growth.

Finally, add a two- to four-inch layer of mulch. You should not use any mulch with large amounts of wood by-products such as redwood or fir bark because they contain tannic acid.

Shading the Root's of Your Clematis

It is often stated that Clematis like to have their feet in the shade and their heads in the sun. It is not so much that the roots need to be in the shade; they are just seeking a ready source of water, which is usually found in the shade.

Shading the roots can be achieved by using a layer of mulch two to four inches thick. Planting annuals or shallow-rooted perennials to cover the Clematis roots will also provide the necessary shade. Do not use stones, rocks or gravel to shade a Clematis's roots. The sun makes these objects extremely hot, which in effect creates an oven where all the heat is captured. This obviously does not create the nice cool root area that is ideal.

Transplanting

Think carefully before planting your Clematis since they are not easy to move. I would not suggest trying to transplant a Clematis after it has been in the ground over five years. The best time to transplant is in the spring or fall.

If you decide to transplant, prepare the new planting site following the procedure I have described earlier in this chapter. Then dig as deeply and as far away as possible from the stem or stems of the plant you are moving. This will allow you to retrieve as much of the rootball as you can. Be careful not to disturb or kink the stem or stems. As you are lifting the Clematis out of the ground, be careful to retain as many of the roots as possible. Keeping the roots intact will reduce the amount of stress being placed on the transplanted plant. After you have moved the Clematis to its new location, water it thoroughly. Use a solution of seaweed extract to help promote root growth.

How to Feed, Water and Mulch Your Clematis

Feeding Your Clematis

A well-fed Clematis is a happy Clematis. As with any plant or animal, proper nutrition is vital to proper growth and health. Regardless of age, a poorly fed Clematis can produce a stunted plant with a crop of inferior flowers. A well-fed, healthy plant is more capable of resisting disease and less susceptible to wilt.

When Should You Start and Stop Feeding Your Clematis

First Feeding

This depends on your weather because the ground temperature needs to be above 55°. This is when your plant becomes active and will need nutrients in order to grow. For those of you that live in warmer winter climate growing zones you will need to start a feeding program sooner than those of you living in colder winter zones because your Clematis will start to come out of dormancy sooner. This all can change from year to year!

Spring feeding should begin when newly developing leaf stems are about one to two inches long. In zones 4 through 9 this usually happens some time in March or April depending upon when the weather starts to warm up.

In zones 10 and 11, this can happen in late February through early March. Although, according to the calendar it may still be winter in zones 10 and 11, springtime conditions can already exist, necessitating this pre-spring feeding.

Final Feeding

In zones 4 through 9, the final feeding of the year should take place in early September. A feeding later than this could stimulate new growth which might not get a chance to harden off prior to the first frost. The cold of winter, especially in an area where the ground freezes, can damage this tender new growth. You need to conserve the plant's energy for springtime when the new growth has a chance to mature.

In zones 10 and 11, if you have Clematis that continue to bloom into November, the final feeding should take place some time between the end of September and early October, depending on climate conditions. But if you live in an area of zones 10 and 11 that experiences a lot of frost, your last feeding should be in early September for the same reasons that apply to zones 4 through 9.

The final application of fertilizer should have a high phosphorous content. This will help flower development in the following season. Do not use a fertilizer which is high in nitrogen. This would stimulate new leaf growth, which is unnecessary at this time of year.

I do not believe it is necessary to fertilize in the winter. The plant is dormant and feeding could stimulate new growth that might be damaged during severe winter conditions. The energy expended by the plant to produce this new growth should be reserved for its normal growth pattern.

What Should I Feed My Clematis

I believe a correct fertilizing program is a very intricate part of *any* plant's overall well being so it is crucial that we adopt a feeding schedule that will not only feed the plant but will also nourish the soil. I have always been an advocate of using environmentally friendly products as often as possible.

As a rule of thumb, any fertilizer that works for roses can be used on Clematis. I personally prefer using fertilizers that contain an organic humus base, beneficial microbes and soil conditioners. This enriches your soil while at the same time feeding your Clematis.

My personal program consists of a fertilizer that is high in phosphorus for my first and last feedings. Between these two feedings, I use the fertilizer with phosphorus and then an all purpose fertilizer alternately. I believe this will be most beneficial for your Clematis and the overall tilth of your garden's soil. By providing your Clematis a healthy soil you will be rewarded with a wonderful crop of blooms.

When feeding your Clematis, follow these recommendations:

● Use the rate of application recommended by the manufacturer of the fertilizer that you use.
● Keep the fertilizer away from the stems of your Clematis to avoid burning them.
● When applying granular fertilizer, be careful not to let the fertilizer touch any of the leaves of the plant. Immediately wash off any excess fertilizer that may land on the foliage. This will prevent burning.
● Always water thoroughly after applying fertilizer.
● Never feed a <u>sick plant</u>. When your plant is ailing is not a good time to stimulate new growth. It needs to use its energy to recover.
● Do not feed a dormant plant.
● <u>Never</u> add lime or manure where the rainfall is light or the soils are alkaline. Both lime and manure contain salts that can ultimately burn the Clematis plant. Lime also inhibits the plant from being able to utilize essential nutrients like iron, manganese and zinc.
● If your Clematis is planted too close to a stucco or cement wall, it will need to have additional minor nutrients like iron, manganese and zinc added to the soil, because, as the materials in these types of walls break down, they turn into lime.

Watering Your Clematis

The important relationship Clematis has with water can never be overstated. Clematis are moisture-loving plants that demand regular amounts of water to prosper.

When watering your Clematis be sure not to overdo it. If a plant receives too much water it can cause rootrot. Clematis will not survive in waterlogged conditions.

Care must also be taken that the crown of their roots is not subjected to constant water. This is another situation that can cause rootrot.

Watering A Newly Planted Clematis

The location you choose to plant your Clematis is an important factor in ensuring that your plant gets an adequate water supply. If a Clematis is planted too close to neighboring shrubs or trees it will be in constant competition for water.

Properly watering your new Clematis, especially in its first year, is _essential_. This is the time when the new Clematis plant is forming the initial stems and root structure that will support it throughout its life.

If you plant your Clematis in the summer, use a minimum of one gallon of water every other day depending upon how well your soil drains. In extreme conditions, water daily if necessary.

Watering Guidelines

Lack of water poses the biggest threat to Clematis during peak growth. The plant is growing so quickly at this time that a constant supply of water is imperative.

An established Clematis requires a minimum of one gallon of water a week but would benefit during active growing periods with up to four gallons or more depending on weather conditions and how well your soil drains.

Some areas of this country have a build-up of concentrated salts from soils and water that are highly alkaline. Deep watering can leach the soil of these accumulated concentrated salts that can be harmful to your plant.

Because of their need for a regular supply of water, it is important during hot, dry periods throughout the year that your Clematis not be allowed to dry out. Clematis consume tremendous amounts of water during these hot spells. They can use several gallons per day depending on the size of the plant and on how well the soil retains moisture.

Do not be fooled by the weather. Even when it rains Clematis still need regular amounts of water. If it rains less than one inch in a seven- to ten- day period, some supplemental watering could be necessary. Do not rely on Mother Nature to do your watering for you. During the fall, start reducing the amount of water you give your Clematis. Even then though, there are exceptions.

In Southern California we can have summer-like temperatures all through fall and even early winter. We also experience what are known as Santa Ana winds. These are strong, gusty winds combined with high temperatures that can have a devastating effect on everything in your garden. If you experience these types of conditions you should use the criteria for summer-like conditions.

Winter is the time to stop your regular watering regimen, but even during this period, *never* allow the plant to dry out completely. Resume regular watering when your Clematis leaf buds start to swell out from their nodes.

Mulching Your Clematis

There are many benefits to applying a layer of mulch to your garden.

A two-to four-inch thick layer of mulch helps the soil retain moisture, thereby cooling the plant's roots. It also limits erosion and helps prevent the soil from compacting.

Mulching discourages weeds because it acts as a barrier, preventing seeds from germinating. It is an ideal environment for earthworms and as it decomposes it helps replenish nutrients in the soil, improving its tilth.

When mulching, apply a two- to four-inch-thick layer of mulch eight to ten inches in diameter around your Clematis. This should be done every spring and again in the fall. Do not let the mulch touch the plant; keep it at least four inches away from its base to prevent rot.

Pruning Your Clematis

There has been a lot written on the subject of the <u>right</u> way to prune Clematis. The fact of the matter is that the plant would continue to bloom each year whether you pruned it or not. If you don't prune, the flowers may not bloom where you want them to. So, the basic goal of pruning is to have your Clematis bloom where you would like it to.

Why You Prune Your Clematis

There are several reasons why you should prune. Probably the main reason most people prune is to enhance their plant's beauty. Pruning removes damaged or weak stems which improves the aesthetics of your plant, and contributes to its well-being.

Beyond that, though, the fringe benefits that accompany pruning are numerous. They include such things as rejuvenating older plants by stimulating new growth. Pruning also increases the ability of your Clematis to bloom. By pruning your Clematis you can contain it, thus allowing you to control its size. Pruning can help to direct and control your plants, which is an effective tool when training them.

Old Wood and New Wood

Before you get your pruning shears out and start clipping away, you need to determine whether you will be working with old wood or new wood.

There is often some confusion when it comes to deciding which wood is old and which is new. It is important to be able to identify one from the other because this will determine which type of pruning you will use.

Old wood is any wood that is more than one year old. It normally looks like a frayed rope, almost as if it were dead. But do not be deceived, it is still a living, vital part of the plant.

New wood is new growth that shoots out of the ground or off existing old wood. It is tender and green.

Flowers always appear on the tips of new stems. The first blooms of the year may appear on short new stems <u>close to the old wood</u>. Even though the blooms appear on new wood, they are still considered to be on old wood because of this close proximity.

However, if the new stems reach a length of several feet or more, and bloom a little later in the growing season, they are considered to be new wood.

When to Prune Clematis

Regardless of which zone you live in, the most important factor in deciding when you should prune your Clematis is when the leaf buds begin to show signs of growth. This is when you should prune. This usually occurs sometime in February or March in zones 4 through 9 and as early as November in zones 10 and 11.

When the leaf buds start growing is determined by the weather and, therefore, can change from year to year depending on climate conditions. You need to keep a watchful eye on the leaf buds so that you do not miss your window of opportunity. By failing to prune at this time, you run the risk of inhibiting flower production.

Light Pruning and Tidy Pruning

Light and tidy pruning are basically interchangeable. They are so similar that I am not going to treat them as two different techniques. The only reason I even mention "tidy" is that you may come across the term in another book.

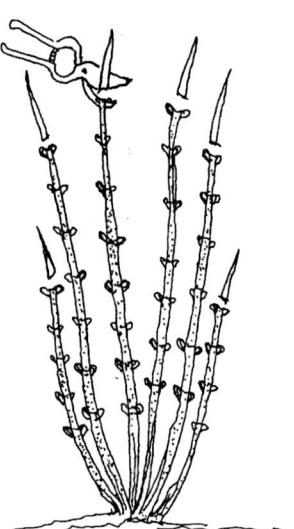

Light pruning is achieved by removing all the dead or damaged wood down to the first pair of healthy leaf buds as in the accompanying illustration. Prune off any dead or brown leaves as well as any old petioles that have not attached themselves to something. Leave the healthy stems at their present height. Reposition the stems so that they will form a neat and attractive vine.

If you accidentally hard prune a Clematis that requires a light prune you would destroy its ability to produce spring or double blooms.

Light Pruning

In fact, light pruning is the <u>only</u> way to prune a double Clematis. If you cut off a stem that produces double flowers you will eliminate its ability to produce these exquisite blooms and sadly end up with just a crop of single flowers.

Hard Pruning

Hard pruning is achieved by cutting back <u>all</u> the stems to a height of twelve to eighteen inches. Make your cut just above a pair of healthy leaf buds.

Clematis varieties that require hard pruning are those that produce flowers on new wood.   Hard pruning is recommended for Clematis varieties that can grow extremely tall. This helps produce a bushier Clematis and eliminates containment problems.

There is an exception to doing a hard prune. Do not prune your Clematis if it has not yet grown to the height that you would like it to be. Just leave it alone until it reaches your desired height.

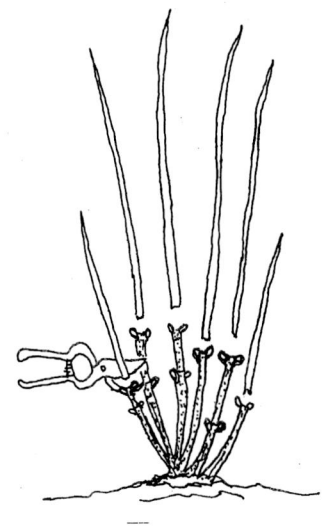

Hard Pruning

To maintain a certain height, measure how much your Clematis grows during the year. This determines its growth potential for the coming year. By pruning back the amount your plant grew in the previous year, you can maintain a desired height. For example, a plant that grew five feet in the previous year should be pruned back five feet this year to maintain that constant height.

Optional Pruning

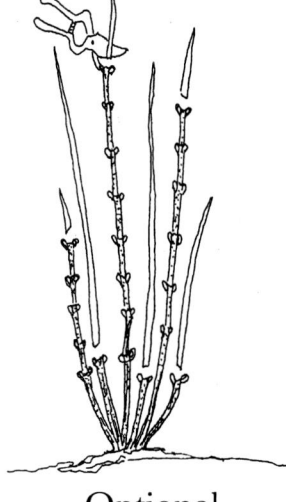

Optional
Pruning

Optional pruning is the best of both worlds because it combines the advantages of both light and hard pruning. It promotes blooms at various heights throughout the vine. It rejuvenates older Clematis that have slowed down its flower production. It allows you to plant hard-pruned Clematis and light-pruned Clematis together. If you are unable to identify which Clematis cultivar you have, pruning it using the optional method is your best bet. This technique leaves some room for error by assuring that should you make a mistake, even with a double Clematis you will not have cut off all of the old wood.

Optional pruning is accomplished by combining both light and hard pruning methods on the same plant. By alternately cutting back half or less of the existing stems each year you can achieve this compromise. The stems you have chosen to prune should be cut to the first pair of healthy leaf buds.

Early Training Requires Some Pruning

If you have purchased a plant smaller than a 5-gallon Clematis you will need to do some initial training. Small or weak stems should be pruned to a height of twelve to eighteen inches. This is done to reduce the strain on the new Clematis's roots by eliminating excess foliage.

Stems should be pruned back to a pair of strong plump leaf buds. I would not recommend pruning stems on Clematis plants that have the potential to produce doubles unless the stems are damaged or weak.

If you have bought a 5-gallon plant as I suggested, early pruning has normally already been done by the wholesaler. Therefore, stems can be either left alone or pruned at your discretion.

To increase flower production in the early stages of your Clematis's life, pinch out the tips of the new shoots that are at least twenty-four inches long. This will encourage side branching, resulting in a fuller plant.

Tidying Tips and Pruning Pointers

- Use a pair of <u>sharp</u> clippers.
- Have a pail for debris and plastic-covered wire ties on hand.
- It is important to take your time and be patient.
- Always start at the top of the stem and work your way down. This eliminates accidentally cutting off too much of a live stem. You can identify a live stem by cutting off a small piece near its top. A live stem will still be greenish inside.
- To increase flower production, remove the seedpods. If you prefer their decorative value, just keep them.
- If your Clematis is a tangled mess you can't unravel, prune just below the problem area. Be brave, this will be painful but necessary. Spread out the remaining stems and re-attach them to their support structure.
- Routinely remove and discard dead, injured or diseased stems and leaves throughout the growing season.
- After you have finished pruning your Clematis it would be beneficial to spray them with a dormant oil. This will suffocate any dormant insect eggs that are waiting for spring to hatch and then feed on your Clematis.

Propagating A Clematis

One of the most frequently asked questions I receive on the Internet is "How do I propagate Clematis?" Propagation is defined as a multiplication or increase, as by natural reproduction. In horticultural terms it is the process of creating a new plant via layering, cuttings or germinating seeds

Gardeners choose to propagate plants for several reasons: to satisfy the challenge of producing their own plant, because the plant is not readily available at their local nursery or because it is a relatively inexpensive way to obtain a duplication of a favorite plant.

I am going to only briefly discuss propagation of Clematis by seeds and cuttings because it is an intricate and lengthy procedure that is covered in many books written on this subject alone. These books give you concise step by step instructions needed for success. There are even college courses that are dedicated to this topic. These courses describe propagation techniques for commercial nurseries as well as home gardeners and show how to do plant propagation by tissue culture, seed, cutting, layering, grafting, and division.

I am very interested in implementing projects in hybridization that would produce *new American cultivars* especially since we presently only have 9 American cultivars. A lifelong desire of mine is to inspire Americans to take on this important challenge and to become actively involved in this area of propagation. Crossbreeding is not an easy operation because it involves careful parent selection and exact timing. It also requires a lot of patience, but I believe the end results are well worth the wait.

Growing Hybrid and Species Clematis by Seed

Growing a hybrid Clematis by seed is most challenging because of the time involved for it to germinate. These little seeds, if they were successfully pollinated, can take anywhere from 18 months to 36 months to germinate. Yes, three years is a long time! But it is also an exciting prospect because these future hybrid Clematis 'babies' do *not* necessarily exhibit any of the same attributes of their mother's flower. These seedlings can often vary in flower color, size, shape and plant vigor. This means, with time, you could potentially be the owner of a unique American Clematis cultivar.

Growing a species Clematis by seed is a much easier procedure. These seeds will produce an offspring just like its mother. They are also much quicker to geminate, some even sprouting in only 30 days.

Both species and hybrid Clematis seeds must be ripe before you gather them. The best time to sow the seed is immediately after it has ripened. This will vary depending on when the flower blooms.

If you would like to try your hand at propagation by seeds here are a few simple guidelines.

It is essential that you are fanatic about your hygienic habits when planting your seeds. This requires you to use a sterilized planting mix that is specifically made for seedlings. Disinfect your containers with horticultural disinfectant or a bleach solution to prevent diseases like damping-off.

Place the planting mix in small 3" containers and cover your seeds with 1/8" of the mix. Moisten and cover with a piece of glass. Place your containers in a shady location such as the north side of your home where the temperature is 60° to 70° or in a cold frame for colder parts of the country. Never allow the soil to dry out completely.

Transplant the sprouted seedlings *carefully* only after they have developed secondary leaves and they are about 2" high. To acclimate them properly move them gradually into a sunny location. Continue to pinch back the tips to promote healthy thick stems. And of course exercise a lot of patience because this is not going to be a fast process.

Propagation by Cuttings

Many gardeners want to share their plants with fellow gardeners and neighbors. This time-honored practice of giving cuttings has gone on for generations. This is reportedly how we now have our American Clematis 'Betty Corning' because when Mrs. Erastus Corning II saw this bell-shaped mauve Clematis in her Albany neighbor's garden, she asked her for a cutting of this pretty little Clematis.

In terms of propagation, taking cuttings from Clematis stems is a more difficult procedure than germinating Clematis seeds. I suggest that it is probably easier if you want a particular Clematis to try and purchase it first for faster enjoyment. However, if taking cuttings is a reproduction technique you would like to try your hand at because you are a die-hard gardener or the Clematis your friend has is not readily available, this is the answer for you.

You will need the following items before you take your cuttings: 6" containers, a sharp clipper or knife, a sterilized planting mix, a rooting hormone that contains a fungicide, labels and large plastic baggies. Before you start you will also need to disinfect your clippers or knife and the containers if they have been used before. Use horticultural disinfectant or a bleach solution to prevent spreading any diseases. You should use a sterilized planting mix that is specifically made for seedlings and for planting cuttings. The manufacturer has already sterilized it and using a heavier mix or native soil would more likely rot out the cuttings. Fill the containers with the planting mix to one-inch below the rim and tamp the mix down lightly. Water thoroughly.

Now you are ready to select your stems for cuttings. The best time to take your cuttings is in the morning hours of summer months. Avoid any sick or weak stems, the very young tips of a Clematis, and stems that are starting to turn brown. You want to select Clematis stems that are healthy, vigorous, green and firm. Take your clippers or knife and cut some appropriate stems. Remove and discard any flowers or growing tips. Cut each stem into three to four inch pieces. Each piece should have one pair leaf joints (node) at the top of the cutting. Cut off one of these of leaves.

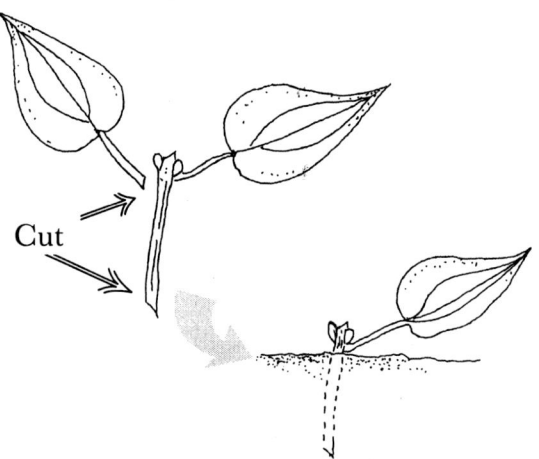

Next, dip the cuttings into a rooting hormone. Be sure to follow the package's instructions *exactly* because these rooting mixtures contain a hormone which, if you put too much on, can actually inhibit it from rooting instead of promoting roots. Use a pencil to make a planting hole. Insert each cutting into a hole and leave the leaf joint (node) uncovered at the top of the soil line. Firm the planting mix around the cutting to eliminate any air pockets. Water again with a fine spray. Label each pot with the cultivar name and date of planting.

Insert four drinking straws or bamboo canes into each pot. Cover the pot with a plastic bag making sure it doesn't touch the leaves. Secure the plastic bag around the pot with a rubber band to maintain a moist, humid atmosphere for your new cuttings so they will not wilt. Place the pot in a warm, bright location in your home, out of any direct sunlight.

Check on your cuttings regularly. Take the plastic bag off daily and turn it inside out to provide ventilation and prevent the build-up of excessive condensation, which can cause the cuttings to rot. Remove and discard any decaying leaves.

Once the cuttings have rooted, in about four to eight weeks, start exposing them to a drier atmosphere by slitting a few openings into the sides of the plastic bag. To check for rooting gently tug on a cutting. Now acclimate these cuttings to the open air by transplanting each cutting into its own pot for about a month. They are finally ready to be exposed to a shaded outside location for another month. Before these new plants will be ready to be planted directly into the ground, they will need to be hardened off for at least a year by leaving them in their containers and gradually exposing them to sunlight. *Good Luck!*

Growing Your Clematis In A Container

When planting your Clematis in a container use one that is a minimum size of 18 inches wide and 18 inches deep. Prior to adding the soil, cover the holes with pieces of screen to prevent the soil from falling through the bottom of your container. This also deters insects from crawling in and taking up residence.

Do not add a layer of gravel, crushed rocks, or charcoal at the base of your container. There are two reasons why I do not recommend doing this. The first reason is that, contrary to popular belief, this custom does not improve drainage. In fact, just the opposite is true. A layer of these materials creates an area that lacks the amount of surface tension that potting soil has. By placing gravel, rock or charcoal in the bottom of your container the gravitational pull is hindered, thus delaying drainage. On the other hand, potting soil's consistent texture allows water to drain more readily by distributing the water evenly. Secondly, these materials displace valuable area that is better utilized by the plant for root growth.

Use a high-grade soilless soil with fast drainage. Place your plant on a layer of soil in your container, making sure that the rootball will be buried 3" to 5" below the soil level. Add soil around the perimeter of the plant and gently tamp it down to eliminate any air pockets. Keep adding soil until you have achieved the desired level of two inches from the rim.

Always leave the original support on your plant until it has acclimated to its new surroundings.

Elevate the container leaving an airspace of at least half an inch. This can be achieved by using small blocks of wood or the terra cotta Pot Feet specifically designed for this purpose. By elevating your container you promote air circulation, which helps prevent water from gathering beneath your pot. An accumulation of water could cause the pot to clog up, inviting root rot.

Every two to three years the Clematis should be completely repotted using all new soil. As with most potted plants, their root systems outgrow their containers and the plant has to be moved to bigger accommodations. The Clematis is no exception. Due to this fact, if you choose to plant more than one Clematis in the same container, it will be necessary to transplant more frequently.

Structures for Container Plants

Clematis grown in a container need some type of support. This can be a trellis, tripod or even an obelisk.

By placing your pot or container near a shrub, an arbor, a fence or other means of support, you increase the number of choices of Clematis plants available to grow in a container.

Feeding and Watering in a Container

A plant in a container is completely dependent upon you for its survival. Because it requires more frequent watering, the nutrients in the potting soil are leached away. These nutrients must be replaced by a regular feeding program.

Start your feeding program either in late winter or early spring, when the leaf buds swell and have grown about one inch long. The final feeding in zones 4 through 9 should be done in the beginning of September. In the more moderate climates of zones 10 and 11, where plants tend to have longer blooming cycles, extend your feeding program through the beginning of October.

Since a plant in a container dries out more rapidly than one in the ground, you need to keep a constant vigil. You cannot rely on natural rainfall to adequately provide your Clematis with the water it needs. You should always check the moisture content to insure that it is properly maintained.

Also, plants in combination are plants in competition. The rootspace, water and food all have to be shared. The only plants I recommend accompanying your Clematis in a container are shallow rooted annuals or perennials because they provide the roots of the Clematis with the shade they need.

Diseases, Insects and Pests

Snails and Slugs

Snails and slugs are among Clematis's worst enemies. They can devour in one night what has taken the Clematis several weeks to produce. There is nothing worse than coming out into your garden and seeing a brand new shoot eaten right to the ground.

One of the best ways to prevent snail damage is to use the copper collar technique. Using copper banding material, form a circular collar around the base of the Clematis. However, this does not prevent snails and slugs from attacking from above or on the sides of a plant that may touch a wall or a fence.

Two other useful means of eliminating these pests are to remove any suspected hiding places that snails and slugs can sleep in during the day, or to handpick them at night. Handpicking requires arming yourself with a flashlight and a pair of rubber gloves so you can hunt, capture and dispose of these slimy predators.

Should you choose chemical warfare, the best defense against snails and slugs is any bait containing the pesticide Metaldehyde. Unfortunately, it is toxic to both cats and dogs, so great care must be taken when using it. There are traps on the market specially designed to contain these toxic snail baits allowing you to protect your pets and children.

Earwigs

Earwigs are omnivorous insects. They tend to eat anything in their path. The damage they do to Clematis can be devastating. They love to bore into unopened flower buds and devour big chunks of the flower's tepals.

Utilizing a trapping program is an effective way to control earwigs. This is done by placing either a piece of PVC pipe, a piece of old hose or a rolled up newspaper on the ground near the Clematis plants that are being attacked. Do this each night before dusk. The earwigs will make these items their home. Go out early the next morning with a pail of hot soapy water and empty the contents of the tubes into the pail. This will ensure that they won't find a new home. Repeat the process until you no longer find any earwigs.

The best chemical product to use against earwigs would be one of the earwig baits on the market that contain the pesticide carabaryl. It is sold as a product called Sevin.

Aphids

Aphids are small green insects that suck the juices out of plants. They can be found on the new leaves and stems of the flowers. Since they feed in great masses they can cause the leaves to curl, discolor and even drop.

Mother Nature has provided us with many beneficial insects that help us fight the battle agianst these predators. These include parasitic wasps, adult ladybugs and the larvae of ladybugs and lacewings.

Sometimes however the aphid population is too large to be controlled by these garden-friendly insects. This over-population usually occurs in the spring before the beneficial insects are out helping you. Only then should you spray to help eliminate the problem. Use a solution of either insecticidal soap or summer oil (also called narrow range oil) to combat the aphids.

Mealybugs

Mealybugs are small insects that look like white cotton candy. They collect along the stems of your Clematis and, like aphids, suck the juices out of the plant. In large numbers, they can cause stunted growth and leaf drop.

The best method of controlling mealybugs is to keep your plant healthy. A weak plant is more susceptible to attack, so keep your plant well watered and well fed.

If a mealybug infestation persists, spray your Clematis with a solution of summer oil (also called narrow range oil) as a means of eradication.

Powdery Mildew

Powdery mildew is a fuzzy, grayish-white, powdery substance that coats tender new leaves and stems. It can cause unsightly deformed flowers and crippled leaves and, in severe cases, reduce flower production. It is a fungus that thrives in shady locations and areas of high humidity. This can pose a real problem for some gardeners on the West Coast.

Powdery mildew's natural enemies are sunlight and good air circulation. Always consider these two factors when planting your Clematis to avoid mildew problems. Spraying your Clematis thoroughly with a dormant oil in winter after pruning prevents the fungal spores from germinating. The dormant oil will suffocate the residual spores that have over-wintered in your plant. Hose off your Clematis leaves once a week in the morning because this dislodges the spores and helps to prevent their development by drowning them.

If the above suggestions do not help, the *best* and *safest* aid in the control of powdery mildew is neem oil. It should be applied when the fungus is first noticed and repeated as necessary. I have had good results with it.

Wilt

The most disappointing problem a Clematis owner can encounter is discovering that a plant has wilt. This is because the ailment strikes quickly without any warning and there is no easy recourse. Clematis are susceptible to several different fungi that can cause them to collapse. These fungi are called wilt because the vine droops and then shrivels. Although this is a serious malady, it is usually not fatal if you have planted your Clematis correctly.

You will know wilt when you see it. First, the uppermost shoots start to go limp, looking as if your Clematis needs water. So you rush to water the plant, thinking this will solve the problem. But then the young foliage starts to turn brown. Finally, the whole stem collapses and dies. This all happens very rapidly. Wilt can occur on only one stem or affect the entire plant.

If you planted your Clematis deep in the first place there is hope for salvation should your plant become infected. Deep planting allows your Clematis to regenerate new growth from below if it is attacked by wilt. A regular watering and fertilizing program to keep your plant healthy is also a strong deterrent to wilt which is more likely to occur if the plant is in a weakened state.

Since the wilt fungus enters your Clematis plant by way of a damaged stem you should always provide adequate support for all new stems. Protecting these fragile new stems from injury will greatly reduce the risk of your Clematis becoming infected with wilt.

Apparently, there is no Clematis that is completely resistant to wilt, but large-flowered hybrids seem to be more susceptible than other varieties. Usually wilt is not a problem for the Clematis viticellas and the Clematis species.

To treat wilt, carefully cut off all of the diseased parts of the vine and then disinfect your clippers. Carefully dispose of all these diseased parts in a trash bag to prevent further spread of these fungi.

Benomyl is one of the only fungicides on the market that addresses Clematis wilt. It is a preventive systemic fungicide and it is not legal in some states. It also has the unfortunate side effect of being lethal to earthworms.

Thankfully, wilt is not usually a problem once the plant has been established for a few years.

Pets

Pets can do damage to your precious Clematis collection as well as to other prized plants you may have in your garden. The family dog or the neighbor's cat can unwittingly trample or jump against the delicate stems, breaking or kinking them and doing severe damage.

If your Clematis is in an area that is susceptible to such an onslaught from the animal kingdom there are a few things you can do for protection. Leave the original stake on the plant, making sure you adjust the ties to allow for the plant's natural growth. A small barrier of three or four bamboo or other sharp or pointed stakes at the base of the plant can also be an effective deterrent. If the problem is severe, a small fence of chickenwire, though unattractive, will do the trick.

Gophers

Gophers are a common garden pest in many areas of the country. They can quickly destroy a plant by devouring its roots. You can keep them away from your most valuable plants by constructing a root guard cage. Since smaller gophers are able to squeeze through chickenwire holes as small as three- quarters of an inch, you should use the smaller half-inch aviary wire to line your planting hole. Ready-made rootguards are available at specialty garden suppliers.

Poisons are another solution, but I do not recommend them for two reasons. Number one, it is difficult to determine if your poisoning program has been effective. You can assume that the problem has been taken care of, but the only way you can be sure is by seeing that your plants haven't been destroyed. This could also lead to unnecessary repeat poison applications.

Number two, the use of poisons around pets and children in the garden can be dangerous.

Using a trap is an effective method and the one I recommend. It gives you the comfort of knowing that you have remedied the problem because, if you are successful, the evidence is right there in the trap.

The Phoenix Phenomenon

"Oh no, my Clematis is dying!"

Imagine your total dismay in finding your once brand-new beautiful Clematis vine has collapsed and certainly looks like it is dead. You are alarmed because you have followed all the planting directions painstakingly, but it still looks as if your beautiful investment is in need of some horticultural CPR. How could this possibly happen? What do you do now? Well, don't call 911 yet.

The answer is that in the <u>first</u> year of growing Clematis, patience is the key. In England gardeners understand and accept that this is a time for nurturing.

Clematis are like the mythological Egyptian bird, the Phoenix, which dies in a fire and later rises renewed from the ashes. Clematis are very resilient plants and most Clematis that have crashed will rejuvenate themselves.

After this apparent demise, they tend to send up even stronger stems than before. For this reason I recommend buying a 5-gallon Clematis. I feel that anything smaller would have a root system too small to generate this rejuvenation, thus greatly diminishing the chances of the Phoenix Phenomenon occurring.

If this catastrophe occurs, treat the plant as if it had wilt, using the procedure described for wilt.

What caused this catastrophe? Why did it happen? Was it Clematis wilt? I do not believe so. It is more likely that one of the plant's fragile stems was somehow kinked, and an adequate supply of water was unable to travel throughout the plant.

Both wilt and blockage of stems can have the same deadly results, a crashed Clematis. The prescription is the same for both, <u>patience</u>. So, when what I call the "Phoenix Phenomenon" occurs, be patient. This rise from the ashes can take from as little as a couple of months to a year or longer.

48 Clematis For Your Garden

Clematis 'Arctic Queen'

Flower Features
The flower's tepals are colored white with a touch of green on the outermost skirt of tepals and form an attractive double rosette. Its stamens are cream-colored. The flower is 4" to 6" in diameter.

Blooms: Early in the season and repeats.
Height Range: Six to eight feet.
Light Exposure: It does well in any exposure.
Prune: Optionally or lightly.

Highlights
This is a remarkable new cultivar. It is an easy-to-grow, repeat bloomer. It blooms double on new wood and is an excellent choice for containers.

Clematis 'Asao'

Flower Features
The flower's tepals are a deep rosy-pink with a white bar in the center. Its stamens are yellow. The flower is 6" to 8" in diameter.

Blooms: Early in the season and repeats.
Height Range: Six to eight feet.
Light Exposure: It is best planted in an area with some shade to prevent the flowers from fading.
Prune: Optionally or lightly.

Highlights
'Asao' blooms early in the season as well as having a very long blooming period. It is a nice compact plant with moderate growth, perfect for growing in a container. It is an ideal Clematis for the shade. It was one of the ACS's Top Ten Clematis for 1997.

Important Note: The following height ranges, blooming periods and flower coloring should be used only as a guideline. How tall a Clematis grows, when and how often it blooms and the intensity of the color has a lot to do with which growing zone you live in and the weather that you experienced that year.

Clematis 'Barbara Jackman'

Flower Features

The flower's tepals are a deep purple with a vivid magenta bar. Its stamens are creamy yellow. The flower is 5" to 7" in diameter.

Blooms: Early in the season and repeats.
Height Range: Six to eight feet.
Light Exposure: It thrives equally in sunny or shady locations.
Prune: Optionally or lightly.

Highlights

'Barbara Jackman' has the advantage of being dramatically colored and still fades gracefully. It is a good choice for growing in a container.

Clematis chrysocoma var. sericea

Flower Features

The flower's tepals are a creamy-white with a slight mauve tinge along the midribs. Its stamens are yellow. The flower is 1 ½" to 2 ½" in diameter and has four cupped tepals.

Blooms: Later in the season.
Height Range: Ten to twenty feet.
Light Exposure: It likes the sun, so plant it in a south, east, or west position.
Prune: Light.

Highlights

Similar in appearance but not to be confused with the Clematis montana, to which it is closely related. The Clematis chrysocoma blooms later in the season than the Clematis montana. It is an excellent choice for a pergola or an arbor.

Clematis 'Comtesse de Bouchaud'

Flower Features
The flower's tepals are a rich, velvety pink with marked midribs.   Its stamens are cream colored. The flower is 4" to 6" in diameter.

Blooms: Later in the season and can repeat.
Height Range: Six to eight feet.
Light Exposure: It thrives equally in sunny or shady locations.
Prune: Optionally or hard.

Highlights
It makes a great Clematis for containers because of its compact nature. It is one of the most popular Clematis with prolific, long-lasting blooms.   It is a versatile pink Clematis that does not tend to fade in the sun.

Clematis crispa

Flower Features
The flower's tepals are a dainty pale blue to lavender-blue and they form a sweet nodding bell. Its stamens are cream yellow.   The flower is 1" to 1 ½" in diameter.

Blooms: Late in the season and repeats.
Height Range: Five to six feet.
Light Exposure: Shade or, if in the sun, with some shelter.
Prune: Optionally or hard.

Highlights
Clematis crispa is a delicate slender vine and should be planted where it can easily be seen.   It has a long blooming period.   Clematis crispa is probably our first American Clematis and it was one of the ACS's Top Ten Clematis for 1998.   It will die to the ground during winter in colder zones.

Clematis 'Daniel Deronda'

Flower Features

The flower's tepals are a striking deep-violet blue. Its stamens are a contrasting ivory color. The flower is 6" to 8" in diameter.

Blooms: Early in the season and repeats.
Height Range: Six to eight feet.
Light Exposure: It will grow in any location but prefers a sunny spot.
Prune: Optionally or lightly.

Highlights

It is a nice compact plant with moderate growth, perfect for growing in a container. When grown in a container it may have semi-double flowers. It is very free flowering.

Clematis 'Dr Ruppel'

Flower Features

The flower's tepals are a strong rosy-pink with a distinct central carmine bar. The later flowers are a little subtler in color. Its stamens are golden. The flower is 6" to 8" in diameter.

Blooms: Early in the season and repeats.
Height Range: Six to ten feet.
Light Exposure: It is best planted in an area with some shade to prevent the flowers from fading.
Prune: Optionally or lightly.

Highlights

It is considered to be one of the best striped Clematis. It is a very popular Clematis because of its vigorous growth and its profuse production of flowers. The central bar of color can vary in width dramatically throughout the season. It was one of the ACS's Top Ten Clematis for 1998.

Clematis 'Duchess of Edinburgh'

Flower Features
The flower's tepals always form a pretty, double rosette and are colored white with a touch of green on the outermost skirt of tepals. Its stamens are cream-colored. The flower is usually 4" in diameter, sometimes reaching 6".

Blooms: Early in the season and repeats.
Height Range: Six to eight feet.
Light Exposure: It does well in any exposure.
Prune: Optionally or lightly.

Highlights
This is a wonderful, time-honored cultivar. It is an easy-to-grow, repeat bloomer. It blooms double on new wood and is an excellent choice for containers. It was one of the ACS's Top Ten Clematis for 1997.

Clematis x 'Durandii'
(syn. Clematis Integrifolia 'Durandii')

Flower Features
The flower's tepals are an indigo-blue. Its stamens are golden-yellow. The flower is 4" in diameter.

Blooms: Early in the season and repeats.
Height Range: Three to five feet.
Light Exposure: It thrives equally in sunny or shady locations.
Prune: Optionally or hard.

Highlights
This Clematis species is a herbaceous sub-shrub. Durandii are non-clinging Clematis, so they need support as they grow. This can be achieved by allowing them to grow into another shrub. It is a free-flowering Clematis. With proper support, it makes a good container selection.

Clematis 'Elsa Späth'
(syn. Clematis Xerxes)

Flower Features
The flower's tepals are a rich violet-blue. Its stamens are reddish-purple. The flower is 6" to 8" in diameter.

Blooms: Early in the season and repeats.
Height Range: Six to eight feet.
Light Exposure: It will grow in any location but prefers a sunny spot.
Prune: Optionally or lightly.

Highlights
It is an easy Clematis to grow and produces flowers for a very long period of time. It was one of the ACS's Top Ten Clematis for 1998.

Clematis 'Ernest Markham'

Flower Features
The flower's tepals are a glowing magenta. Its stamens are golden-yellow. The flower is 4" to 6" in diameter.

Blooms: Late in the season and repeats.
Height Range: Eight to ten feet.
Light Exposure: It performs best when planted in an area with some direct sun light.
Prune: Optionally or lightly.

Highlights
It is a time-honored and popular Clematis because it produces a nice profusion of flowers.

Clematis 'Fairy Queen'

Flower Features

The flower's tepals are the most delicate shade of pink with a soft rosy-mauve bar.   Its stamens are dusty purple.   The flower is 6" to 9" in diameter.

Blooms: Early in the season and repeats.
Height Range: Six to eight feet.
Light Exposure: It is best planted in an area with some shade to prevent the flowers from fading.
Prune: Optionally or lightly.

Highlights

It is exceptionally large and free-flowering with attractively formed blooms.   It is an excellent choice for a container or a small patio garden. It has a very long blooming period.

Clematis 'General Sikorski'

Flower Features:

The flower's tepals are a pretty near-blue with a hint of red at the base of each tepal. Its stamens are golden.   The flower is 6" to 8" in diameter.

Blooms: Early in the season and repeats.
Height Range: Six to eight feet.
Light Exposure: It will grow in any location but prefers a sunny spot.
Prune: Optionally or lightly.

Highlights:

It is a vigorous grower.   Its compact nature makes it well suited for growing in containers.

Clematis 'Gillian Blades'

Flower Features
The flower's tepals are a pure white but when they first open the tepals are blushed with a tinge of mauve. Its stamens are yellow. The flower is 6" to 9" in diameter.

Blooms: Early in the season and repeats.
Height Range: Six to eight feet.
Light Exposure: It thrives equally in sunny or shady locations.
Prune: Optionally or lightly.

Highlights
Gillian Blades is a beautiful refined white Clematis. It is a prolific and trouble-free Clematis. It would make a good container selection.

Clematis 'Gipsy Queen'

Flower Features
The flower's tepals are a rich, velvety purple. 'Gipsy Queen' is often mistaken for a 'Jackmanii', but its distinct cutouts at the base of the tepals can easily identify it. Its stamens are wine-colored. The flower is 4" to 6" in diameter.

Blooms: Later in the season and repeats.
Height Range: Eight to twelve feet.
Light Exposure: It thrives equally in sunny or shady locations.
Prune: Optionally or hard.

Highlights
It is an excellent choice because it is very free-flowering and a vigorous performer. Take advantage of its height by growing it with another tall Clematis or a climbing rose. I like it because of its great performance and its attractive tapered tepals.

48 Clematis For Your Garden

Clematis 'H. F. Young'

Flower Features

The flower's tepals are a bright mid-blue often described as Wedgwood Blue. Its stamens are yellow. The flower is 6" to 8" in diameter.

Blooms: Early in the season and repeats.
Height Range: Six to ten feet.
Light Exposure: It likes the sun, so plant it in a south, east, or west position.
Prune: Optionally or lightly.

Highlights

It is a very popular Clematis, and deservedly so, because of its exceptional color and free-flowering ability. It is an excellent choice for a container or a small patio garden. It was one of the ACS's Top Ten Clematis for 1997.

Clematis 'Hagley Hybrid'

Flower Features

The flower's tepals are a speckled shell pink. Its stamens are brown. The flower is 4" to 6" in diameter.

Blooms: Later in the season and repeats.
Height Range: Six to eight feet.
Light Exposure: It grows well in the shade. It is one of the few pink varieties that can tolerate a mild eastern or western exposure.
Prune: Optionally or hard.

Highlights

It blooms later in the season and is rarely without flowers. It is easy to grow and is a great choice for a container.

48 Clematis For Your Garden

Clematis 'Henryi'

Flower Feature
The flower's tepals are a distinct creamy-white. Its stamens are brown. The flower is 6" to 8" in diameter.

Blooms: Early in the season and repeats.
Height Range: Eight to ten feet.
Light Exposure: It thrives equally in sunny or shady locations.
Prune: Optionally or lightly.

Highlights
It is one of the oldest Clematis and it may even be one of the first hybridized Clematis. It is still very popular and has withstood the test of time.

Clematis integrifolia 'Rosea'

Flower Feature
The flower's tepals are a mauve pink and forms a bell-shaped flower. Its stamens are yellow. The flower is 1 1/2" in diameter.

Blooms: Later in the season and repeats.
Height Range: Two to three feet.
Light Exposure: It does best when planted in full sun.
Prune: Hard.

Highlights
Clematis integrifolia 'Rosea' is a non-climbing plant. It makes an excellent border plant.

Clematis 'John Huxtable'

Flower Feature
The flower's tepals are colored a translucent white. Its stamens are cream-colored. The flower is 4" to 6" in diameter.

Blooms: Later in the season and repeats.
Height Range: Eight to ten feet.
Light Exposure: It thrives equally in sunny or shady locations.
Prune: Optionally or hard.

Highlights
It is a free-flowering cultivar. It is an excellent Clematis to combine with other hard-prune varieties. Because of its compact size it is suitable for a container. It was one of the ACS's Top Ten Clematis for 1998.

Clematis 'Kathleen Dunford'

Flower Feature
The flower's tepals form a semi-double flower that is a deep and speckled rosy-purple. This is a unique semi-double consisting of two overlapping layers. Its stamens are red. The flower is 7" to 9" in diameter.

Blooms: Early in the season and repeats.
Height Range: Six to nine feet.
Light Exposure: It thrives in sunny locations.
Prune: Optionally or lightly.

Highlights
It is an excellent choice for a container or a small patio garden. It has a very long blooming period. It was the number one choice of the ACS's Top Ten Clematis for the year 1998.

48 Clematis For Your Garden

Clematis 'Lady Betty Balfour'

Flower Feature
The flower's tepals are a deep violet. Its stamens are a distinctive contrasting-yellow. The flower is 6" to 8" in diameter.

Blooms: Later in the season.
Height Range: Eight to fifteen feet.
Light Exposure: It does best when planted in full sun where its intense color can be appreciated.
Prune: Optionally or hard.

Highlights
It is a tall cultivar that makes an excellent choice for a pergola or an arbor. 'Lady Betty Balfour' is both trouble-free and vigorous. Another nice feature is that this Clematis blooms later on in the year for summer or fall color.

Clematis 'Lord Nevill'

Flower Feature
The flower's tepals are a rich deep blue with pretty undulating edges. Its stamens are purple. The flower is 6" to 8" in diameter.

Blooms: Early in the season and repeats.
Height Range: Six to eight feet.
Light Exposure: It will grow in any location but prefers a sunny spot.
Prune: Optionally or lightly.

Highlights
It is long-time favorite and beautiful Clematis and has a good crop of repeat flowers. Lord Nevill and Masquerade would be an excellent combination to grow together. It was one of the ACS's Top Ten Clematis for 1998.

Clematis 'Madame Baron Veillard'

Flower Feature
The flower's tepals are a velvety lilac-pink.   Its stamens are white.   The flower is 4" to 6" in diameter.

Blooms: Early in the season and repeats.
Height Range: Eight to ten feet.
Light Exposure: It does best when planted in full sun.
Prune: Optionally or hard.

Highlights
It is free-flowering and vigorous.   It makes an excellent choice for a pergola or an arbor.

Clematis 'Madame Grange'

Flower Features
When the flower opens its tepals are a breath-taking velvety carmine.   As it ages it turns a dusky purple.   Its stamens are beige. The flower is 4" to 6" in diameter.

Blooms: Later in the season and repeats.
Height Range: Eight to twelve feet.
Light Exposure: It thrives equally in sunny or shady locations.
Prune: Optionally or hard.

Highlights
This is an exquisite, time-honored cultivar.   It is a vigorous and free-flowering Clematis.   Its cupped tepals make a nice contrast to the flat shape of most other Clematis.

Clematis 'Marie Boisselot'
(syn. Clematis 'Madame Le Coultre')

Flower Features
The flower's tepals are a spectacular pure white. Its stamens are pale yellow.   The flower is 6" to 9" in diameter.

Blooms: Early in the season and repeats.
Height Range: Eight to sixteen feet.
Light Exposure: It thrives equally in sunny or shady locations.
Prune: Optionally or lightly.

Highlights
It is a very free-flowering and vigorous Clematis. It is considered to be one of the best large white cultivars of Clematis.   It was on the ACS's Top Ten Clematis list for 1997.   Even though the flower is quite large, the tepals are well formed and hold up nicely.

Clematis 'Margaret Hunt'

Flower features
The flower's tepals are a dusky mauve-pink.   Its stamens are coffee-colored.   The flower is 4" to 6" in diameter.

Blooms: Later in the season and repeats.
Height Range: Eight to twelve feet.
Light Exposure: It thrives equally in sunny or shady locations.
Prune: Optionally or hard.

Highlights
Take advantage of its height by growing it with another tall Clematis or a climbing rose.   It is a vigorous Clematis.   Though the flowers are relatively small for a hybrid, they make up for this shortcoming with their abundance.

Clematis 'Masquerade'

Flower Features
The flower's tepals are a soft lavender with a darker center bar. Its stamens are wine red. The flower is 6" to 8" in diameter.

Blooms: Early in the season and repeats.
Height Range: Six to eight feet.
Light Exposure: It thrives equally in sunny or shady locations.
Prune: Optionally or lightly.

Highlights
It was one of the ACS's Top Ten Clematis for 1997. It is loved for its dramatic coloring and ruffled tepals. Its compact size makes it an excellent container selection.

Clematis 'Nelly Moser'

Flower features
The flower's tepals are a subtle mauve-pink with a deep carmine bar. Its stamens are maroon. The flower is 7" to 9" in diameter.

Blooms: Early in the season and repeats.
Height Range: Six to ten feet.
Light Exposure: It is best planted in an area with some shade to prevent the flowers from fading.
Prune: Optionally or lightly.

Highlights
It is probably the second best known Clematis cultivar behind Clematis 'Jackmanii'. The popularity of this Clematis is based on its repeat blooming ability and vigor.

Clematis 'Niobe'

Flower Features
The flower's tepals are a velvety ruby-red, but as they open they emerge nearly black. Its stamens are light yellow. The flower is 4" to 6" in diameter.

Blooms: Early in the season and repeats
Height Range: Six to eight feet.
Light Exposure: It performs best when planted in an area with some direct sun.
Prune: Optionally or hard.

Highlights
Its profuse blooming ability and distinctive color make it an exceptional Clematis. It is a good container cultivar. It is one of the best red Clematis because its color holds so well.

Clematis 'Proteus'

Flower Features
This double Clematis is capable of producing up to 100 frilly tepals. They are a soft mauve-pink. The stamens are yellow. The flower is 6" to 8" in diameter.

Blooms: Early in the season and repeats.
Height Range: Six to eight feet.
Light Exposure: It thrives equally in sunny or shady locations.
Prune: Optionally or lightly.

Highlights
This older Clematis is grown for its eye-catching double flowers. It deserves more recognition than it receives because of its outstanding free-flowering performance. It was one of the ACS's Top Ten Clematis for 1997. It makes an excellent container selection.

48 Clematis For Your Garden

Clematis 'Snow Queen'

Flower Features
The flower's tepals are snow-white with delicate mauve-pink bars. The flowers face skyward.   Its stamens are a deep reddish-brown.   The flower is 6" to 8" in diameter and has rippled edges.

Blooms: Early in the season and repeats.
Height Range: Eight to ten feet.
Light Exposure: It thrives equally in sunny or shady locations.
Prune: Optionally or lightly.

Highlights
It is an elegant white free-flowering Clematis.   It makes an excellent container selection.

Clematis 'Star of India'

Flower Features:
The flower's tepals are a striking reddish-plum with a carmine central bar.   Its stamens are yellow.   The flower is 4" to 6" in diameter.

Blooms: Later in the season and repeats.
Height Range: Twelve to twenty feet.
Light Exposure: It thrives equally in sunny or shady locations.
Prune: Optionally or hard.

Highlights
Star of India is admired for its stunning coloration.   This is a Clematis that is grown for its late continuous display of blooms.   It makes an excellent choice for a pergola or an arbor.   It was one of the ACS's Top Ten Clematis for 1997.   It is a free-flowering and vigorous Clematis.

Clematis tangutica

Flower features

The flower's tepals are a bright yellow and form a lantern-shaped flower.   Its stamens are brown. The flower is 1" to 1 $\frac{1}{2}$" in diameter.

Blooms: Later in the season and repeats.
Height Range: Can grow to twenty feet.
Light Exposure: It thrives equally in sunny or shady locations.
Prune: Optionally(if space allows) or hard.

Highlights

It has wonderful feathery seedpods that can be used in floral arrangements.   It is a very vigorous species Clematis.

Clematis texensis
'Duchess of Albany'

Flower Features:

The flower's tepals are a pretty satiny-pink with a central cherry-red bar.   Its stamens are yellow.   The flower is 2" to 3" in diameter.

Blooms: Later in the season and repeats.
Height Range: Eight to ten feet.
Light Exposure: It will grow in any location but prefers a sunny spot.
Prune: Optionally or hard.

Highlights

This is a unique Clematis because of its four tepals that form tulip-like flowers that face skywards.   It is an easy texensis to grow.

Clematis texensis 'Gravetye Beauty'

Flower features
The flower's tepals are a bright crimson-red. Its stamens are yellow.   The flower is 2 ½" to 3" in diameter.

Blooms: Early in the season and repeats.
Height Range: Six to ten feet.
Light Exposure: It will grow in any location but prefers a sunny spot.
Prune: Optionally or hard.

Highlights
'Grav. B.' comes closest of all Clematis to a genuine red color.   Its trumpet shaped tepals ultimately open up to a star-like flower.

Clematis 'Victoria'

Flower Features
The flower's tepals are a soft rosy-purple with three midribs and a textured surface.   Its stamens are cream colored. The flower is 4" to 6" in diameter.

Blooms: Later in the season and can repeat.
Height Range: Eight to sixteen feet.
Light Exposure: It thrives equally in sunny or shady locations.
Prune: Optionally or hard.

Highlights
Victoria is one of the easiest Clematis to grow and the most dependable.   It is a real workhorse. I would highly recommend it for all gardens in hot locales.   It was the number one choice of the ACS's Top Ten Clematis for the year 1997.   It is a very vigorous Clematis that blooms profusely.

Clematis 'Ville de Lyon'

Flower Features
The flower's tepals are a deep carmine-red on the outer edges with a crimson bar in the center. Its stamens are a creamy-yellow that make an interesting contrast.   The flower is 4" to 6" in diameter.

Blooms: Later in the season and can repeat.
Height Range: Eight to twelve feet.
Light Exposure: It will grow in any location but performs best in a sunny location.
Prune: Optionally or hard.

Highlights
It performs vigorously and will bloom throughout the summer.   The coloring of 'Ville de Lyon' is both beautiful and unique.   It was one of the ACS's Top Ten Clematis for 1998.

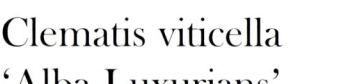

Clematis viticella 'Alba Luxurians'

Flower features
The flower's tepals are a creamy-white with green tips and they form nodding cupped flowers.   Its stamens are dark purple.   The flower is 2 ½" to 3 ½" in diameter.

Blooms: Later in the season and repeats.
Height Range: Eight to twelve feet.
Light Exposure: It thrives in the sun but will grow in any position.
Prune: Optionally or hard.

Highlights
It makes an excellent choice for a pergola or an arbor in hot locales.   It was one of the ACS's Top Ten Clematis for 1998.

Clematis 'Betty Corning'

Flower Features

The flower's tepals are a soft lavender-mauve and form a small nodding bell.   Its stamens are yellow. The flower is 1 ½" to 2" in diameter.

Blooms: Later in the season and repeats.
Height Range: Eight to ten feet.
Light Exposure: It grows best with an east, west, or south exposure but will also grow in the shade.
Prune: Optionally or hard.

Highlights

It makes an attractive combination when grown with another viticella or hard-pruned large-flowered hybrid.   This first Clematis developed in America was named for Mrs. Erastus Corning II, who was a board member on the New York Botanical Garden.   It now has the distinction of being one of the best American cultivars.

Clematis viticella 'Madame Julia Correvon'

(syn. Clematis 'Madame Julia Correvon')

Flower features

The flower's tepals are a clear wine-red.   Its stamens are golden-yellow.   The flower is 3" to 4" in diameter.

Blooms: Early in the season and repeats.
Height Range: Six to eight feet.
Light Exposure: It thrives in the sun but will grow in any location.
Prune: Optionally or hard.

Highlights

This is a very popular viticella and a good performer.   This viticella is a good selection for containers because it is so compact.   It is often listed in books as a large hybrid flowering Clematis because it has such large blooms.

Clematis viticella 'Polish Spirit'

Flower Features

The flower's tepals are a rich velvety-purple. Its stamens are reddish brown. The flower is 2 ½" to 3 ½" in diameter.

Blooms: Later in the season and repeats.
Height Range: Ten to fifteen feet.
Light Exposure: It thrives in the sun but will grow in any location.
Prune: Optionally or hard.

Highlights

It is an outstanding new cultivar destined to be a classic. It was one of the ACS's Top Ten Clematis for 1997. It has a large profusion of blooms over an extended period of time. It is heat tolerant and a great choice for first-time Clematis gardeners.

Clematis viticella 'Venosa Violacea'

Flower Features

The flower's tepals are a soft creamy-white and are outlined with a deep violet margin with purple veins. Its stamens are green. This combination of colors is very striking. The flower is 4" in diameter.

Blooms: Later in the season and repeats.
Height Range: Ten to fifteen feet.
Light Exposure: It thrives in the sun but will grow in any location.
Prune: Optionally or hard.

Highlights

It is one of the largest and most attractive of the viticellas. As with all viticellas it is easy to grow and it is also heat tolerant.

Clematis 'Vyvyan Pennell'

Flower Features
The flower's tepals are a beautiful deep-violet blue.   Its stamens are golden.   The flower is 6" to 8" in diameter.

Blooms: Early in the season and repeats.
Height Range: Six to eight feet.
Light Exposure: It does best in the sun.
Prune: Optionally or lightly.

Highlights
It is capable of producing semi-double and double blooms on old wood.   'Vyvyan Pennell' is an exquisite Clematis.   Often called 'Queen of the Clematis', it is one of the best of the double cultivars.

Clematis 'Walter Pennell'

Flower features
The flower's tepals are a unique deep mauve-pink streaked with a darker bar.   Its stamens are buff-colored.   The flower is 6" to 8" in diameter.

Blooms: Early in the season and repeats.
Height Range: Six to eight feet.
Light Exposure: It does best when planted in the full sun.
Prune: Optionally or lightly.

Highlights
It is capable of producing semi-double and double blooms on old wood.   It is a nice compact plant with moderate growth, perfect for growing in a container.   It is very free-flowering and would be an excellent choice to be grown with Vyvyan Pennell.

Clematis 'Will Goodwin'

Flower features
The flower's tepals are a very pretty pale lavender-blue. Its stamens are creamy- white. The flower is 6" to 8" in diameter.

Blooms: Later in the season and repeats.
Height Range: Six to eight feet.
Light Exposure: It thrives equally in sunny or shady locations.
Prune: Optionally or lightly.

Highlights
It is a nice compact plant with moderate growth, perfect for growing in a container. It was one of the ACS's Top Ten Clematis for 1998.

Clematis 'William Kennett'

Flower Features
The flower's tepals are a rich lavender-blue with a subtle reddish-purple stripe down the center. Its stamens are dark purple. The flower is 7" to 8" in diameter.

Blooms: Early in the season and repeats.
Height Range: Eight to twelve feet.
Light Exposure: It thrives equally in sunny or shady locations.
Prune: Optionally or lightly.

Highlights
It is one of the first Clematis cultivars and is still very popular. 'William Kennett' is an exceptional performer and is prized for being one of the most trouble-free and continuously flowering Clematis. This heat-tolerant Clematis was one of the ACS's Top Ten Clematis for 1997.